The China Village Stir Fry Cookbook

V O L U M E   2

CHINA VILLAGE

Published by:
Keilen, Ltd.
A division of Joyce Chen, Inc.
6 Fortune Drive,
Billerica, MA 01821,
U.S.A.

Model # 97-0075T

Printed in Taiwan

Acknowledgements
—Design and typesetting by Clara Graves Graphic Design
—Recipes by Helen Chen. Additional recipes by Susan Slack.
—Cover Design by Meyers Associates

CONTENTS

GETTING READY TO COOK

Introduction 5
The Right Equipment 6
China Village Stir Fry Sauces and Oils 8
Stir Frying and Other Cooking Methods 9
Oriental and Western Ingredients from Your Market 11
How to Serve a Chinese Meal 14

BEEF & LAMB DISHES

Chinese Spaghetti 17
Stir-Fried Beef with Red Bell Peppers 18
Beef with Broccoli in Szechuan Sauce 19
Beef with Mushrooms 20
Shredded Ginger Beef 20
Spicy Stir-Fried Steak Cubes 21
Lamb with Scallions 22

PORK DISHES

Steamed Meatballs with Water Chestnuts 24
Barbecued Sesame Ribs 25
Stir-Fried Spicy Pork Shreds with Carrots 26
Braised Pork with Vegetables 27
Stir-Fried Pork with Cabbage and Black Mushrooms 28
Chinese Pork Chops 29

CHICKEN DISHES

Crispy Chicken Nuggets 31
Sweet & Sour Chicken 32
Chinese Roast Chicken 33
Lemon Chicken with Pine Nuts 34
Szechuan Chicken with Peanuts 35
Spicy Orange Chicken Wings with Sesame Seeds 36
Chicken with Zucchini and Walnuts 37
Sliced Chicken with Chinese Vegetables 38
Steamed Curried Chicken 39

SEAFOOD DISHES

Seafood Medley in Crispy Noodle Nest	41
Bird's Nest Noodles	42
Szechuan Shrimp with Pea Pods	42
Shrimp with Lobster Sauce	43
Lemon Scallop Stir Fry	44
Pan-Fried Salmon with Spicy Lemon Sauce	45
Szechuan Clams with Black Bean Sauce	46
Steamed Whole Fish	47
Red Snapper with Broccoli and Black Mushrooms	48

VEGETABLES AND SALADS

Stir-Fried Chinese Cabbage	50
Bean Sprout, Ham and Carrot Salad	50
Szechuan Spiced Eggplant	51
Stir-Fried Vegetable Medley	52
Steamed Eggplant Salad	52
Stir-Fried "Kan Shao" Green Beans	53
Fried Bean Curd with Broccoli	54
Lemon Cucumber Salad	55
Fresh Asparagus Salad	55
Crunchy Chinese Chicken Salad	56

NOODLES, RICE AND DUMPLINGS

Stir-Fried Noodles with Shredded Pork	58
Chinese Soup Noodles with Sliced Beef	59
Cold Spiced Chinese Noodles	60
Almond Fried Rice	61
Spicy Meat-Filled Dumplings	62
Szechuan Dipping Sauce	63
Noodles Tossed with Spicy Beef	64

WELCOME TO THE CHINA VILLAGE COLLECTION

We hope you will enjoy the *China Village Stir Fry Cookbook, Volume 2*. Stir frying is a Chinese art form that has come down through the ages, and with each generation it becomes even better.

Stir frying is the brisk cooking of small cuts of meats, vegetables, poultry or seafood in small amounts of cooking oil over intense heat. The quick cooking helps to retain vitamins and minerals found naturally in all foods.

Stir frying is easy, even for the beginner. Once you understand and follow the basic techniques explained on the following pages, you'll find yourself stir frying on a regular basis. It's a quick, simple and inexpensive way to prepare delicious, nutritious meals that fit perfectly with today's busy lifestyles and desire for healthy eating.

Stir frying opens up an almost unlimited variety of dishes to serve by mixing and matching your favorite sauces, meats, seafood and vegetables. The beauty of this method is that you can cook as easily for eight people as you can for just one or two. These recipes are likely to become family favorites that are served for many years to come.

GETTING READY TO COOK:
THE RIGHT EQUIPMENT

Chinese Kitchen Knife

A good knife is the most important tool in the kitchen, especially so in the Chinese kitchen, where ingredients are cut with precision to create various sizes and shapes for stir frying. The most important preparation is finished before the cooking begins! The China Village Chinese Kitchen Knife is a traditional Chinese chef's knife with a high-carbon, stainless steel blade and a round, hardwood handle. This handsome knife is weighted and balanced for effortless cutting and slicing. It is a valuable tool for both the novice and experienced cook.

Stir Fry Pans

The China Village Stir Fry Pan comes in 9 ½-inch and 12-inch diameter sizes, in either pro-weight carbon steel or non-stick finishes. The pan was designed to be smaller, more compact and easier to use on a Western stove than the traditional, round-bottom, 14-inch wok. The special flat bottom fits more securely on top of the home stove. A single long handle provides the cook with superb balance. The stir fry pan can be used for a variety of cooking tasks such as stir frying, deep frying, pan frying and steaming. It doubles as a skillet and is excellent for pan frying. The non-stick version does not require seasoning. Less oil is required for stir frying, which is a plus for people on low-fat diets.

Woks

The China Village line offers a 14-inch traditional wok made from heavy-gauge carbon steel for fast, efficient heat conduction and a flat bottom for today's modern kitchens. A skillet-type handle and side helper allows safe, convenient handling. Use the wok often and season it regularly to develop a black patina on the inside surface and prevent rusting. For the busy cook, we recommend the non-stick model. This wok doesn't require seasoning and cleanup is fast. Like the stir fry pan, less oil is required for stir frying. Boxed sets are available in either finish. These sets include a wok, a lid, spatula and stir fry recipe booklet.

Bamboo Stir Fry Tools

Our well-shaped Bamboo Stir Fry Tools feel comfortable in the hand. The rounded spatula matches the contour of the rounded stir fry pan or wok. It will not damage the finish of non-stick cookware. Bamboo is stronger and more durable than wood. It will not swell, fray or split. Bamboo stir fry tools can go into the dishwasher.

Bamboo Steamer

Steaming is a healthful cooking technique that accentuates the natural flavor of foods. Our China Village 10-inch Bamboo Steamer is handmade from natural bamboo. The handsome 3-piece set consists of two tiers for holding foods, and a lid. It is designed to sit over a stir fry pan or wok filled with boiling water. Bamboo absorbs condensation from steaming, thus preventing soggy foods.

Microwave Rice Cooker

Rice is a staple food in the Chinese kitchen. The handy China Village Microwave Rice Cooker has a generous 2-quart capacity and prepares perfectly cooked rice. It will free up your stove top burner for wok cooking. The rice cooker can go directly from the microwave to the table. Dishwasher safe, the unit is also great for steaming vegetables.

Dumpling Press

Made from high impact plastic, our versatile China Village Dumpling Press will shape Chinese dumplings or those from other cuisines: Italian raviolis, Spanish empañadas, Polish pierogis and Jewish kreplachs. With the Dumpling Press, you can easily seal dozens of sweet or savory stuffings inside thin pastries to create appetizers, desserts and snacks.

Skimmer

The China Village Brass Skimmer features a sturdy, brass wire basket and a long bamboo handle. It is indispensable for blanching or poaching. It is the perfect tool for scooping up fried foods such as spring rolls or wontons. Excess oil drains from the food back into the pan through the open-weave basket. Or, remove noodles and dumplings from boiling water. You will find yourself reaching for this handy tool every day!

Folding Fry Racks

These handy racks have folding "fences" that fold up for holding larger amounts of fried food than the ordinary flat tempura racks. The sides fold down for easy storage. China Village Folding Fry Racks are available in 12-inch or 14-inch sizes.

Dinnerware Set

China Village offers an authentic 12-piece Chinese blue and white dinnerware set. It includes four porcelain bowls, four porcelain spoons and four sets of carved, metal-tipped chopsticks. You will enjoy serving your delicious Chinese foods in these beautiful dishes.

CHINA VILLAGE STIR FRY SAUCES AND OILS

The China Village stir fry sauces and stir fry oil will give your dishes an authentic Chinese restaurant taste. The common denominator for all Chinese cooking is soy sauce. **China Village Szechuan Stir Fry Sauce** and **Spicy Lemon Stir Fry Sauce** are made from custom-blended, high-quality Chinese soy sauce, infused with seasonings and spices to create our one-step cooking sauces. These sauces are excellent all-purpose seasonings for Chinese dishes. You can use them interchangeably in any Chinese recipe that calls for soy sauce. It is not necessary to add additional seasonings to your Chinese dishes, but if you prefer a hotter, spicier taste, we recommend adding a dash or two of Mexican Fiesta Chile Pepper Oil from our companion line of Mexican cookware and accessories.

Szechuan Stir Fry Sauce

Adapted from a classic Chin dynasty sauce known as "Kung Pao," our China Village Szechuan Stir Fry Sauce is blended with natural seasonings and hot spices indigenous to the Szechuan province. It is an excellent all-purpose seasoning for any type of meat, seafood or vegetable dish. Use as a marinade, in dipping sauces or to add flavor depth to sauces, soups or salads. This spicy, zesty sauce will also add a piquant touch to many Western style dishes. *(10-ounce bottle)*

Spicy Lemon Stir Fry Sauce

The flavor of fresh lemons gives our China Village Spicy Lemon Stir Fry Sauce its subtle, tangy taste. Although not as spicy as the Szechuan Stir Fry Sauce, it can be used interchangeably. A wonderful marinade or cooking sauce. *(10-ounce bottle)*

China Village Garlic & Ginger Stir Fry Oil

Custom-blended, this aromatic oil has been flavored with natural garlic and ginger. It is made with 100% canola oil and contains no cholesterol. This healthy oil has a light texture and is excellent for stir frying. It adds a delicious combination of garlic and ginger to meats, vegetables, poultry and seafood dishes. You can also use it for preparing popcorn, and as a flavoring oil in marinades, salad dressings or sauces. *(8-ounce bottle)*

China Village Sweet & Sour Dipping Sauce

This tangy condiment is made from a blend of apricots, apples and natural cider vinegar. Serve it with chicken wings or nuggets, egg rolls, spare ribs, Chinese pastries or meatballs. It also makes an excellent glaze for poultry and roasts. *(8-ounce bottle)*

STIR FRYING
AND OTHER COOKING METHODS

Stir Frying

Stir frying is very easy. Follow these suggestions for an enjoyable cooking experience. First, cut and prepare everything *before* you start to cook. Cut ingredients into bite-size pieces and marinate if necessary.

Don't add everything into the wok at one time. The rule of thumb is to add ingredients in the order in which they will cook, with slower-cooking vegetables going into the pan first. Often, ingredients are cooked separately for total control, and then combined together at the end. This way, you ensure that the tender ingredients don't overcook and the larger pieces are not undercooked.

Next, have everything well organized so that you don't have to interrupt the stir-frying operation by having to measure out or look for ingredients while you're cooking.

And finally, get to know the characteristics of different ingredients so you can adjust the heat and timing, as needed. This way, you don't just follow recipes; you learn to interpret them.

It's so easy that once you begin you'll wonder why you never stir-fried before. It's the easy way to cook, especially when you use tools made with the quality and precision that make China Village a true standard of excellence in Oriental cuisine.

Steaming

Steaming is an ancient Chinese cooking method that is almost as popular as stir frying. Fill a stir fry pan or wok with ample water, yet not enough to touch the food. Place over medium-high heat. Place food in a plate or shallow pan to catch the juices. The plate should fit inside the bamboo steamer yet leave 1 to 2 inches space for steam to circulate. When the water boils, set the covered steamer filled with food into the stir fry pan. Replenish the boiling water, if necessary.

When removing the covered steamer from the stir fry pan, wear cooking mitts to protect your hands from hot steam and resulting painful burns.

After the cooking process, the bamboo steamer will retain heat and keep foods warm about 30 minutes. Attractive, basketlike bamboo steamers double as serving containers and can be placed directly on the dinner table.

Deep Frying

Chinese cooks have long prepared foods through deep frying. Today, cooks often avoid deep frying in the interest of reducing fat in the diet, but properly prepared deep-fried foods can be an occasional treat. If they are quickly sealed by the hot oil, foods should not be greasy. They will retain their juicy interiors, turning crisp and golden brown.

Use a flat-bottom stir fry pan or wok when deep frying. This will ensure that the oil-filled wok sits securely on the stove top and does not tip over. Because of the contours of the stir fry pan or wok, less oil is needed for deep frying.

Deep fry with a vegetable oil low in saturated fat. Peanut oil, corn oil or safflower oil are good choices. The oil temperature should be from 350° to 375°F. Test oil with a deep-fat thermometer or drop in a piece of bread. If the bread turns golden brown in 65 seconds, the oil is at 350°.

Cut foods into uniform-size pieces. Do not overload the pan. If necessary, adjust heat as foods are added to the oil. Foods fried at too low a temperature absorb oil and become greasy. Drain foods well on a wire rack or paper towels.

ORIENTAL AND WESTERN INGREDIENTS FROM YOUR MARKET

The Chinese are adventurous, creative cooks. For centuries, they have been willing to experiment with and consume almost anything edible. Food markets in today's China are filled with exotic and unusual vegetables. In their special approach to cooking, one fact remains apparent. Whichever ingredients are used, Chinese cooks demand they be the freshest available.

Quality ingredients are essential to preparing delicious Chinese dishes. Stir-fried vegetables are quickly cooked so they must be fresh, and the meats you select should be tender cuts. Try to select fish that haven't been frozen. Whole fish should be firm and bright eyed, with no slimy feel to the skin. Stir frying brings out the best of each ingredient, but it will not mask poor-quality ingredients.

Happily, markets throughout the country have developed a new awareness of special Chinese ingredients, thanks to the large influx of immigrants. Fresh ginger root, wonton skins, pea pods and bok choy can be found in the produce section of almost any large food store. Sesame oil, hoisin sauce and oyster sauce are easily found on the dry goods shelves in the Oriental food section. If you live near a large Asian population, you will be able to find a larger variety of Asian foodstuffs in your local markets. Produce stands and farm markets offer a top-quality selection of fresh produce. Try to utilize fruits and vegetables at the peak of their season.

A visit to your local supermarket will allow you to put this food philosophy to work in your kitchen and create many of China's culinary masterpieces. Your local supermarket should provide you with enough raw materials to create all the recipes in this book and dozens more. Substitutes are suggested if an item might be difficult to find. Prepare perishable items as soon as possible after they are delivered to your kitchen. Serve the finished dishes quickly after they are prepared.

Using Cornstarch

You will notice that cornstarch is used in almost all stir fry recipes. Cornstarch is used by the Chinese as a thickener. It makes a clear sauce and is a faster cooking thickener than flour.

Generally, cornstarch should not be added dry to the food you are cooking as this will result in one nasty lump. Mix cornstarch with water and have it ready to add at the end of stir frying to thicken the sauce as needed. Usually 1 or 2 teaspoons of cornstarch in 1 to 2 tablespoons cold water is sufficient. Add it slowly, judging the thickness of the sauce as you stir.

The cornstarch that you add directly to raw meats and seafood is used to help hold in and seal the natural juices. Have you ever cooked beef and then looked to your amazement to find the food swimming in liquid? That's the juices that have been released from the beef; the dish will be watery and the beef dry. Stir frying raw beef mixed with cornstarch will help to avoid this problem.

There is no hard, fast rule on quantity since it depends on what you are cooking. Some ingredients such as mushrooms and bean curd release large amounts of water when cooked—they need a bit more cornstarch. Other ingredients with smaller amounts of moisture, such as carrots, require less. How much cornstarch to use will come from experience. What if you miscalculate? If you didn't use enough, mix a little more cornstarch with a small amount of water and add until the gravy has the right consistency. If you've used a bit too much, add some water or broth and stir to thin it out.

A problem with cornstarch is that it has a tendency to stick. The solution is not to add more oil, but to use a little bit of water or broth to help dissolve the clinging cornstarch. This liquid also helps to make nice gravy. You should always add water cautiously, one tablespoon at a time. You'll find this "water" technique useful in that it will result in a much less oily taste.

Using Hot Chilis

If you like spicier food, you may wish to use hot chilis to make your dishes taste hotter. Since the small seeds from dried chilis are not especially attractive in a finished dish, remove the seeds before cooking.

Using a pair of scissors, snip off a small portion of the stem and cut the chili open on one side. With the scissors blade you can scrape away the seeds; they will fall out easily. Discard the seeds and use the chili pod only.

To use, stir fry the chili pods in oil that is just starting to get hot. If your oil is too hot, the dried chilis will burn before their hot oils are "coaxed" out. Stir the chilis in the oil for a few seconds and then remove, or you can leave them in for added flavor and continue with the recipe. You may wish to ultimately remove the chili pods from the finished dish so that an unsuspecting guest will not accidentally eat one! You may make the recipes in this book spicier by using this method. Or you can add hot chili oil to taste directly to food during or after cooking.

Cooking Temperatures

Most of the recipes use medium-high heat. This is because with the reduced amount of oil, the heat needs to be slightly lower to start. This helps to prevent the food from sticking to the pan.

It is difficult to say exactly which temperature (low, medium, high) to use since everyone's stove is different. The rule of thumb is to start out at medium-high and adjust up or down accordingly. If the food is burning or sticking, lower the temperature. If the food is not sizzling properly, increase the temperature.

Most stoves, especially electric, do not give instantaneous response. You may prefer to use the technique of lifting the pan from the heat source to reduce the heat and replacing it when more heat is needed. This up and down motion is easier and more efficient than constantly adjusting the heat, and basically provides immediate response. Try it. When the pan is lifted away from the heat, the cooking slows down. You may also move the pan onto a cool burner. This enables you to continue stirring while the pan cools.

HOW TO SERVE A CHINESE MEAL

The Chinese eat family style. They prepare a number of dishes (usually one dish per person) and place them in the center of the table. This, of course, depends upon the size of each dish and the appetite of the eaters. A meal for four adults could be three to four main dishes with a soup.

Everyone has his or her own bowl of hot, steaming rice and a pair of chopsticks. Each diner partakes of the various dishes and accompanies the food with bites of rice.

Westerners eat far less rice than the Chinese. This is why Americans complain of being hungry soon after a Chinese meal. They don't eat enough rice!

Variety is the spice of life—and it applies to eating too. When you are planning a Chinese meal, think about variety and don't prepare three meat dishes. It is far better to make one meat, one seafood and one vegetable dish.

The Chinese usually hold a bowl of rice to their mouth and gently push the rice in. Westerners find this particularly difficult to do. And no wonder—they have been trained from childhood that it is bad manners to hold a bowl or plate to one's mouth. For the Chinese, this is perfectly acceptable and makes eating rice much easier. Try it!

How to Use Chopsticks

Now that you have set your table with Chinese porcelain and have served authentic Chinese food, what about using those chopsticks?

Chopsticks are wonderful tools. They are commonly made of wood or bamboo and do not conduct heat or alter the taste of certain spices. Fancy chopsticks can be made from such diverse materials as ivory, enamel, sterling silver or lacquerware. Chinese chopsticks have blunt ends, while Japanese chopsticks are pointed.

Bamboo or wood chopsticks are good for beginners. They are not as slippery. Follow the diagram on the next page.

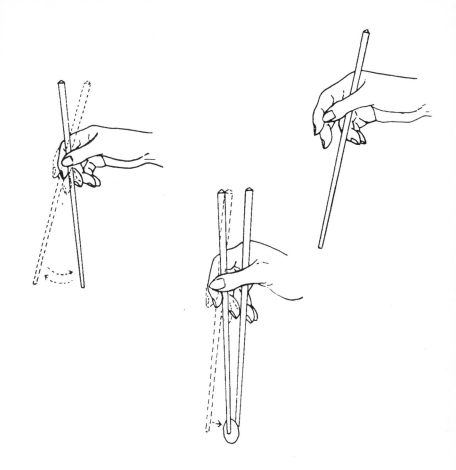

Held and used in the correct way, the bottom chopstick should remain stationary while only the top chopstick moves. If you have difficulty at first, just keep practicing.

Remember you are using muscles in your hand you usually do not use. Be patient and you'll succeed. It might help to use a large napkin as a bib the first few times you use chopsticks. You'll be glad you did.

CHINA VILLAGE

BEEF

AND

LAMB

DISHES

CHINESE SPAGHETTI

Toss this spicy meat mixture with your favorite thin spaghetti-style noodles, or serve portions over steaming rice. For a spicy-hot flavor, add a little Mexican Fiesta Chile Pepper Oil.

¾ pound ground beef or pork
3 Tablespoons China Village Szechuan Stir Fry Sauce
¼ cup chicken broth or water
1 heaping Tablespoon hoisin sauce or brown bean sauce
1 teaspoon cornstarch
3 Tablespoons China Village Garlic & Ginger Stir Fry Oil, divided
4 Tablespoons minced scallion, divided
1 teaspoon grated ginger root
1 clove garlic, minced
¼ cup minced water chestnuts
2 black mushrooms, soaked, stems removed and minced
½ pound fresh Chinese noodles or ¾ pound dried noodles
1 cucumber, seeded and julienned

Marinate meat with stir fry sauce. In a small bowl, combine chicken broth, hoisin sauce and cornstarch. Set aside.

Heat 2 Tablespoons oil in a stir fry pan or wok over medium-high heat. Stir fry 2 Tablespoons scallion, ginger root, garlic, water chestnuts and mushrooms 1 minute. Add meat; stir fry until no longer pink. Add chicken broth mixture; stir until ingredients are well combined and glazed. Set aside.

Cook noodles according to package directions. Drain; toss with remaining 1 Tablespoon oil. Arrange on a platter; top with meat sauce and remaining scallion. Toss noodles to serve. Garnish each portion with cucumber. Serve warm.

Yield: 2 to 3 servings

STIR-FRIED BEEF WITH RED BELL PEPPERS

This colorful dish features sweet, ripe red bell peppers and spicy-hot chile pepper oil. You can substitute yellow or green peppers for the red ones.

¾ pound flank steak

2 Tablespoons China Village Szechuan Stir Fry Sauce

1 Tablespoon dry sherry

2 teaspoons cornstarch

½ teaspoon sugar

dash of ground black pepper

3 ½ Tablespoons China Village Garlic & Ginger Stir Fry Oil, divided

1 teaspoon grated ginger root

1 small red onion, cut into 1-inch pieces

2 red bell peppers, seeded, cut into 1-inch pieces

4 medium black mushrooms, soaked, stems removed, quartered

water or beef broth, as necessary to prevent sticking

½ teaspoon Mexican Fiesta Chile Pepper Oil, or to taste

Cut beef across the grain into slices ¼-inch thick and about 2 inches long. In a medium bowl, combine meat, stir fry sauce, sherry, cornstarch, sugar and black pepper.

Heat 1½ Tablespoons oil in a stir fry pan or wok over medium-high heat. Stir fry ginger root and onion 30 seconds. Add bell peppers and mushrooms; cook 1 minute. Remove vegetables to a serving platter.

Heat 2 Tablespoons oil in the pan over medium-high heat. Stir fry meat 1 to 2 minutes, until no longer pink. Add a splash of water or broth to help prevent sticking. Return vegetables to pan. Drizzle in chile pepper oil. Toss ingredients together. Scoop onto serving platter; serve hot.

Yield: 3 to 4 servings

BEEF WITH BROCCOLI IN SZECHUAN SAUCE

A variation on an old favorite that will please everyone.

1 pound flank steak
4 Tablespoons China Village Szechuan Stir Fry Sauce
1 Tablespoon cornstarch
3 stalks fresh broccoli (about 4 cups or 1 pound)
3 Tablespoons China Village Garlic & Ginger Stir Fry Oil, divided
¼ cup water or beef broth

Cut beef across the grain into thin slices, ⅛-inch thick and about 2 inches long. Mix beef with stir fry sauce and cornstarch and set aside.

Cut broccoli into florets about 2 inches long. Peel the stalks and slice into 2-inch lengths, about ½-inch thick.

Heat 1 Tablespoon oil in stir fry pan or wok over medium-high heat. Add broccoli and stir fry for 30 seconds. Add water or broth to pan and cover, stirring occasionally, until broccoli turns dark green, about 2 minutes. Remove from pan and spread out on a plate.

Heat remaining 2 Tablespoons oil in same pan over medium-high heat. Stir in beef mixture and keep stirring until almost done. If meat begins to stick to the pan, add a few tablespoons of water or broth while stirring. Return broccoli to pan and stir fry for 1 minute. Serve hot.

Yield: 4 to 6 servings
Variation: Use China Village Spicy Lemon Stir Fry Sauce

BEEF WITH MUSHROOMS

Mushrooms naturally make food taste better. For a little variety try using different kinds of mushrooms such as Chinese black mushrooms or canned straw mushrooms.

1 pound flank steak

3 Tablespoons soy sauce

1 Tablespoon cornstarch

1 Tablespoon dry sherry

1 teaspoon sugar

4 Tablespoons China Village Garlic & Ginger Stir Fry Oil, divided

8 ounces fresh mushrooms (about 4 cups)

1 slice ginger root or ¼ cup sliced onion

Cut beef across the grain into thin slices, ¼-inch thick by 2 inches long. Mix sliced beef with soy sauce, cornstarch, sherry and sugar and set aside.

Cut fresh mushrooms into slices ¼-inch thick.

Pour 2 Tablespoons oil in stir fry pan or wok over high heat. Add mushrooms and stir fry until mushrooms wilt, about 2 minutes. Remove mushrooms from pan and set aside.

Heat remaining 2 Tablespoons oil in same pan over high heat. Add ginger or onion slices. Add beef mixture and stir fry until done, about 2 minutes. Add cooked mushrooms to the beef mixture and mix thoroughly. Serve immediately.

Yield: 4 to 6 servings

SHREDDED GINGER BEEF

Succulent stir-fried beef and fresh ginger are a winning combination!

1 pound flank steak

3 Tablespoons China Village Szechuan Stir Fry Sauce

1 Tablespoon cornstarch

1 teaspoon sugar

1 teaspoon sesame oil

dash of ground black pepper

2 Tablespoons oyster sauce

2 Tablespoons dry sherry or water

3 Tablespoons China Village Garlic & Ginger Stir Fry Oil

3 or 4 paper-thin slices peeled ginger root, cut into fine shreds

2 thin scallions, cut into 1-inch diagonal shreds

⅓ cup fresh cilantro leaves

Cut beef across the grain into thin slices, ⅛-inch thick and about 2 inches long. Stack several slices at a time; cut into shreds.

In a medium bowl, combine beef shreds, stir fry sauce, cornstarch, sugar, sesame oil and black pepper.

In a small dish, mix oyster sauce and sherry; set aside.

Heat oil in a stir fry pan or wok over medium-high heat. Stir fry ginger root and scallions for 30 seconds. Add beef and stir fry for 1 to 2 minutes, or until no longer pink. Sprinkle in oyster sauce mixture. Add cilantro. Stir fry about 30 seconds longer. Scoop onto a serving platter and serve hot.

Yield: 4 servings

SPICY STIR-FRIED STEAK CUBES

East meets West in the flavor of this succulent, easy-to-prepare steak dish. Serve fried rice, or a baked potato and green salad on the side.

1 pound tender beef steak, trimmed, cut into 1-inch cubes

¼ cup China Village Szechuan Stir Fry Sauce

2 teaspoons Worcestershire sauce

⅓ teaspoon ground black pepper

2 Tablespoons China Village Garlic & Ginger Stir Fry Oil

1 large clove garlic, minced

2 teaspoons butter or margarine

1 minced scallion

In a medium bowl, combine beef, stir fry sauce, Worcestershire sauce and black pepper. Marinate 10 minutes.

Heat oil in a stir fry pan or wok over medium-high heat. Stir fry beef and garlic for 1 minute, until medium-rare or until meat reaches desired degree of doneness. Stir in butter. Remove to a serving platter and garnish with scallion. Serve hot.

Yield: 4 servings

LAMB WITH SCALLIONS

Hoisin sauce is available in the ethnic section of most large supermarkets or at any Chinese market.

1 pound boneless leg of lamb or shoulder chops
4 Tablespoons China Village Szechuan Stir Fry Sauce
2 Tablespoons hoisin sauce
6 stalks scallions, about 4 cups
3 Tablespoons China Village Garlic & Ginger Stir Fry Oil or
cooking oil
1 clove garlic, crushed

Cut lamb across the grain into slices 2 inches by 1½ -inches, about ⅛-inch thick. Mix with stir fry sauce and hoisin sauce. Set aside.

Split white bulbous end of scallions with a knife and cut both the green and white parts into 2-inch lengths. Set aside.

Heat oil in stir fry pan or wok over medium-high heat. Add garlic and stir fry 30 seconds, then stir in lamb mixture. Stir fry for 30 seconds, or until lamb is partially cooked.

Add scallions, and continue stirring until scallions wilt and turn a darker green and the meat is done. Serve hot.

Yield: 4 to 6 servings

CHINA VILLAGE

PORK

DISHES

STEAMED MEATBALLS WITH WATER CHESTNUTS

Serve these flavorful meatballs with rice or cooked noodles to capture every delicious drop of sauce. Leftover meatballs are delicious re-steamed.

4 teaspoons cornstarch, divided
2 thin scallions, minced
3 Tablespoons China Village Szechuan Stir Fry Sauce, or to taste
1 teaspoon grated ginger root
1 clove garlic, minced
½ cup finely diced water chestnuts
Dash of ground black pepper
1 pound lean ground pork or beef

In a medium bowl, blend 3 teaspoons cornstarch and half the scallions with remaining ingredients. Shape mixture into meatballs, about 1 inch in diameter. Place in an 8-inch round baking pan.

In a stir fry pan or wok, bring water to boil. Place pan of meatballs on steamer rack; add cover. Place over boiling water; cook 15 to 20 minutes until done. Remove steamer rack from pan. Break open a meatball to be certain the pork is cooked. If not, steam a few more minutes. Remove meatballs to a warm platter.

In a small saucepan, thicken pan juices with the remaining teaspoon cornstarch mixed with 1 Tablespoon water. You can enhance the flavor of the sauce by stirring in 2 or 3 teaspoons stir fry sauce. Pour hot sauce over meatballs and garnish with remaining scallions. Serve hot.

Yield: 4 to 6 servings

BARBECUED SESAME RIBS

Make plenty of these succulent ribs and be sure and pass lots of napkins! The recipe can be easily doubled.

⅓ cup China Village Szechuan Stir Fry Sauce

3 Tablespoons hoisin sauce

3 Tablespoons brown sugar

1 clove garlic, minced

2 Tablespoons dry sherry

½ teaspoon Chinese five-spice powder

1 rack of young pork spareribs, about 2 to 3 pounds

2 teaspoons sesame seeds

Maple syrup, to taste

In a large, shallow baking pan, blend stir fry sauce, hoisin sauce, brown sugar, garlic, sherry and five-spice powder. Coat ribs in mixture; refrigerate 2 hours or overnight.

Preheat oven to 375°. Drain ribs; place on a rack in a foil-lined roasting pan. Sprinkle ribs with sesame seeds. Roast 40 minutes; turn and roast 20 minutes more. Turn ribs again. Cook 10 minutes or until meat shrinks away from the end of the rib bones.

Remove from oven; brush lightly with maple syrup. Cut into individual ribs for serving.

Yield: 2 to 3 servings

STIR-FRIED SPICY PORK SHREDS WITH CARROTS

Save time and cut down on the preparation by purchasing a package of long julienne strips of carrots in the produce section of your market.

¾ pound thinly sliced, lean boneless pork, shredded

3 Tablespoons China Village Szechuan Stir Fry Sauce

2 teaspoons cornstarch

½ teaspoon sugar

3 Tablespoons China Village Garlic & Ginger Stir Fry Oil, divided

2 medium carrots, cut into long julienne strips

3 small scallions, smashed, shredded

3 Tablespoons chicken broth or water

1 teaspoon Mexican Fiesta Chile Pepper Oil, or to taste

In a medium bowl, combine pork with stir fry sauce, cornstarch and sugar. Marinate 30 minutes.

Heat 1 Tablespoon oil in a stir fry pan or wok over medium-high heat. Stir fry carrots 1 minute. Add scallions and stir fry 1 minute more. Remove vegetables to a serving platter.

Heat stir fry pan with remaining oil. Stir fry pork 3 minutes, or until no longer pink.

Stir in carrots and chicken broth. Drizzle in chile pepper oil; mix well. Serve hot.

Yield: 4 servings

Technique: Smashing and Shredding

Some recipes in this cookbook may call for green onions, sliced ginger root or unpeeled garlic to be smashed or crushed before use. Lay the vegetable on a cutting board. With the broad side of a cleaver or a chef's knife, hit it with a firm whack. The fibers will be broken and the vegetable flattened. Juices will be released, providing more flavor. It will be easier to cut the green onions into long thin threds using the tip of a knife. Garlic skins will loosen and can be easily removed.

BRAISED PORK WITH VEGETABLES

Serve this delicious pork, vegetables and sauce in a large bowl over rice. The flavor is even better if the dish is cooked in advance, then reheated.

about 2 pounds pork shoulder or butt
2½ cups chicken broth or water
¼ cup China Village Szechuan Stir Fry Sauce
1 Tablespoon brown sugar
2 scallions, cut into 1-inch pieces
2 thin slices ginger root, crushed
3 medium carrots, cut into ¾-inch pieces
6 to 8 ounces small white mushrooms

Trim pork of excess fat. Cut into large chunks. To remove additional fat, blanch pork in boiling water 5 minutes. Discard blanching water.

In a medium saucepan, combine chicken broth, stir fry sauce, brown sugar, half the scallions and the ginger root. Add pork. Cover and simmer 1 hour. If sauce reduces too much, add a little more broth.

Place carrots and mushrooms on top of pork. Cover; cook 20 minutes or until meat and vegetables are tender. Put pork and vegetables into a serving bowl. Mince remaining scallions; sprinkle on the top. Serve hot.

Yield: 5 to 6 servings

STIR-FRIED PORK WITH CABBAGE AND BLACK MUSHROOMS

The meat will be easier to thinly slice if partially frozen.

1 pound lean boneless pork

3 Tablespoons China Village Szechuan Stir Fry Sauce

1 Tablespoon cornstarch

¼ cup chicken broth

1 Tablespoon oyster sauce

1 teaspoon sugar

4 Tablespoons China Village Garlic & Ginger Stir Fry Oil, divided

3 stalks Chinese cabbage, sliced diagonally into 2-inch pieces

4 medium black mushrooms, soaked, stems removed and quartered

2 small scallions, cut into 1-inch pieces

Cut pork into pieces ¼ inch thick and about 2 inches long. In a small bowl combine pork with stir fry sauce and cornstarch. In another small bowl, blend chicken broth, oyster sauce and sugar; set aside.

Heat 2 Tablespoons oil in a stir fry pan or wok over medium-high heat. Add cabbage and stir fry 1 minute. Add mushrooms and scallions; stir fry 1 minute more. Remove vegetables to a platter.

Heat 2 Tablespoons oil in the stir fry pan over medium-high heat. Stir fry pork 3 minutes, or until no longer pink. Pour in broth mixture and stir until meat becomes glazed. Mix in reserved vegetable mixture. Serve hot.

Yield: 3 to 4 servings

CHINESE PORK CHOPS

Any remaining sauce can be served as a thin gravy over rice—it is delicious!

3 Tablespoons China Village Szechuan Stir Fry Sauce
¼ cup water
1 teaspoon light brown sugar
1 Tablespoon China Village Garlic & Ginger Stir Fry Oil
1 pound thin-cut boneless pork chops
1 cup sliced onions

Mix stir fry sauce, water and brown sugar in a small bowl; set aside.

Heat oil in a stir fry pan or wok and heat over medium-high heat. Place pork chops in pan and brown on both sides. Remove chops to plate, reserving as much oil as you can in the pan. Stir fry sliced onion in the same pan over medium-high heat, until light golden brown.

Return pork chops to pan and pour in sauce mixture. Allow sauce to come to a boil, and then reduce heat to medium. Cover and cook slowly for about 5 minutes.

When thoroughly cooked, place chops on a deep serving platter.

Yield: 4 to 6 servings
Variation: Use China Village Spicy Lemon Stir Fry Sauce

CHINA VILLAGE

CHICKEN

DISHES

CRISPY CHICKEN NUGGETS

Scented with fresh ginger, these crispy chicken bites will be a hit at your next party. Serve them with a bowl of tangy China Village Sweet & Sour Sauce for dipping.

2 whole chicken breasts, skinned, boned and cut into 1-inch cubes
2 Tablespoons China Village Szechuan Stir Fry Sauce
1½ teaspoons grated ginger root

BATTER

1 cup all-purpose flour, divided
¼ cup cornstarch
½ teaspoon baking powder
¼ teaspoon salt
¾ cup cold water
vegetable oil for deep-frying

1 bottle China Village Sweet & Sour Dipping Sauce

In a small bowl, mix cubed chicken with stir fry sauce and ginger root. Refrigerate 30 minutes.

In a medium bowl, whisk together ½ cup flour, cornstarch, baking powder, salt and cold water.

Heat 2 inches of oil in a stir fry pan or wok over medium-high heat to 375° for deep-frying.

Place remaining flour on a plate, and dust chicken cubes in the flour. Place about one-third of the chicken cubes at a time into the batter. Fry several pieces at a time for 3 to 4 minutes, or until crispy and medium golden brown. Drain on paper towels.

Place cooked chicken nuggets on a large serving platter with a bowl of sweet & sour sauce in the center for dipping. Serve hot.

Yield: 6 to 8 servings
Variation: Use China Village Spicy Lemon Stir Fry Sauce

SWEET & SOUR CHICKEN

The crispy chicken pieces are served on top of the sauce to help prevent sogginess.

1 recipe Crispy Chicken Nuggets, page 31
1 Tablespoon China Village Garlic & Ginger Stir Fry Oil
1 small green pepper, seeded and cut into 1-inch pieces
1 small onion, cut in wedges
1 large clove garlic, minced
½ cup pineapple cubes or canned lychee fruit
1 bottle China Village Sweet & Sour Dipping Sauce

Prepare Crispy Chicken Nuggets as directed in the recipe on page 31. Drain well and keep warm in a 200° oven.

Heat oil in a stir fry pan or wok over medium-high heat. Stir fry green pepper, onion and garlic for 1 to 2 minutes. Reduce heat to low. Stir in pineapple and the whole bottle of sweet & sour sauce.

Pour hot vegetable-sauce mixture into serving platter. Arrange chicken on top. Serve hot.

Yield: 4 to 5 servings

CHINESE ROAST CHICKEN

The chicken is delicious sliced, or hand-shredded for use in other dishes.

1 broiler-fryer, about 3½ pounds, rinsed
¼ cup China Village Szechuan Stir Fry Sauce
1 Tablespoon dry sherry
2 Tablespoons honey
3 thin slices ginger root, crushed
2 thin scallions, cut into 1-inch pieces
¼ cup chopped fresh cilantro
China Village Garlic & Ginger Stir Fry Oil, as needed, or
*   vegetable oil*

Place chicken and all the remaining ingredients inside a large, plastic zipper bag with a tight-fitting seal. Place secured bag in a shallow pan; refrigerate overnight. Turn bag 1 or 2 times.

Preheat oven to 375°. Remove chicken from bag; place on a rack in a heavy roasting pan. Pat skin dry; brush with oil. Add a little water to the pan. Stuff the ginger root and scallions inside the cavity of the chicken.

Roast 60 minutes or until chicken is glistening brown and the drumstick moves easily. Let chicken rest 20 minutes before carving.

Yield: 3 to 4 servings
Variation: Use China Village Spicy Lemon Stir Fry Sauce

LEMON CHICKEN WITH PINE NUTS

This recipe is a delicious Western adaptation from the Chinese collec-
tion of sweet & sour dishes. It is pretty served on a bed of stir-fried pea
pods.

2 whole chicken breasts, skinned and boned
2 Tablespoons China Village Spicy Lemon Stir Fry Sauce
2 Tablespoons dry sherry
1 cup chicken broth
⅓ cup fresh lemon juice
¼ cup sugar
1 teaspoon grated lemon rind
¼ teaspoon salt
2 Tablespoons cornstarch
1 teaspoon sesame oil
4 Tablespoons China Village Garlic & Ginger Stir Fry Oil
½ cup cornstarch, or as needed
¼ cup toasted pine nuts, as garnish
1 thinly sliced lemon, as garnish

With a heavy rolling pin, pound chicken to slightly flatten. Marinate
with stir fry sauce and sherry.

In a small saucepan, combine broth, lemon juice, sugar, grated
lemon rind, salt, cornstarch and sesame oil. Stir over medium-high heat
until mixture comes to a boil and thickens. Keep warm.

Heat stir fry oil in a stir fry pan or large skillet over medium-high
heat. Dust chicken with cornstarch. Sauté on both sides for 10 to 15
minutes, or until done. (If necessary, add additional oil to keep chicken
from sticking to pan.)

Drain chicken on paper towels, then slice across the grain.

Arrange chicken slices in their original breast shape on a serving
platter. Pour the sauce over chicken. Garnish with pine nuts and lemon
slices. Serve hot.

Yield: 4 to 5 servings

SZECHUAN CHICKEN WITH PEANUTS

Also known as "Kung Pao Chi Ting," this is a classic Szechuan dish. You can make it as hot as you like by adding fresh or dried chili peppers.

2 chicken breasts, skinned, boned and diced into ¾-inch pieces

4 Tablespoons China Village Szechuan Stir Fry Sauce

1 Tablespoon cornstarch

3 Tablespoons China Village Garlic & Ginger Stir Fry Oil

water or chicken broth, as necessary to prevent sticking

½ cup unsalted peanuts

Mix diced chicken with stir fry sauce and cornstarch.

Heat oil in a stir fry pan or wok over medium-high heat. Add chicken mixture and stir fry until almost cooked, about 2 minutes. If necessary, add a few tablespoons of water or chicken broth to prevent the chicken and cornstarch from sticking.

Add peanuts and stir fry 1 minute. Serve immediately.

Yield: 4 to 6 servings

Variation: Use China Village Spicy Lemon Stir Fry Sauce

If you like spicy food, fry several hot dried chilis in the oil before adding chicken (add as many chilis as you want for the hotness you desire). To keep the dish looking attractive, cut each chili open with a pair of scissors and remove all the seeds before frying. Be sure to remove the chili peppers before serving so no one will eat them accidentally—they are very hot.

SPICY ORANGE CHICKEN WINGS WITH SESAME SEEDS

Easy cleanup; fantastic flavor! The chicken wings can also be cooked outdoors over a hot charcoal grill.

3 pounds chicken wings, about 15 pieces
½ cup China Village Szechuan Stir Fry Sauce
2 Tablespoons brown sugar
Grated rind of 1 medium orange
1 large clove garlic, minced
1 Tablespoon sesame seeds

Rinse wings. In a large plastic zipper bag with a tight-fitting seal, combine stir fry sauce, brown sugar, orange rind and garlic. Add wings; coat well in mixture. Place bag in a shallow pan; refrigerate overnight or up to 2 days. Turn bag 1 or 2 times to marinate wings evenly.

Preheat oven to 375°. Pour off marinade and discard. Place wings in a baking pan; sprinkle with sesame seeds. Roast 40 minutes, turning once or twice, until mahogany-brown and crisp. Remove to serving platter. Serve hot or cold.

Yield: 3 to 4 appetizer servings

Variation: Use China Village Spicy Lemon Stir Fry Sauce, and substitute the grated rind of a medium lemon for the orange rind.

CHICKEN WITH ZUCCHINI AND WALNUTS

The rich taste and texture of crunchy, toasted walnuts compliments the flavorful stir-fried chicken and squash.

2 whole chicken breasts, skinned, boned, cut into ¾-inch pieces

3 Tablespoons China Village Szechuan Stir Fry Sauce

1 Tablespoon cornstarch

2 Tablespoons hoisin sauce

1 Tablespoon chicken broth or water

3 Tablespoons China Village Garlic & Ginger Stir Fry Oil, divided

2 small zucchini, halved lengthwise, cut into ½-inch pieces

2 thin scallions, cut into ½-inch pieces

½ cup sliced water chestnuts

1 large clove garlic, minced

½ cup toasted walnuts

In a large bowl, combine chicken with stir fry sauce and cornstarch. In a small bowl, combine hoisin sauce with broth; set aside.

Heat 1 Tablespoon oil in a stir fry pan or wok over medium-high heat. Stir fry zucchini and scallions 1 minute. Add water chestnuts and garlic; stir fry 1 minute more. Remove to serving platter.

Heat 2 Tablespoons oil in pan. Stir fry chicken about 3 minutes or until no longer pink. Stir in vegetables. Add hoisin sauce mixture; mix all the ingredients together. Pour into serving platter; garnish with walnuts. Serve hot.

Yield: 4 to 5 servings

Variation: Use China Village Spicy Lemon Stir Fry Sauce

SLICED CHICKEN WITH CHINESE VEGETABLES

Slice everything about the same size and shape for a consistency in appearance and cooking time.

> *2 whole chicken breasts, skinned, boned and cut into thin slices*
>
> *2 teaspoons cornstarch*
>
> *3 Tablespoons China Village Szechuan Stir Fry Sauce*
>
> *4 Tablespoons China Village Garlic & Ginger Stir Fry Oil, divided*
>
> *1 slice ginger root*
>
> *¼ cup scallion, cut into 1½-inch lengths*
>
> *½ cup sliced bamboo shoots, drained*
>
> *½ cup black mushrooms, soaked, stems removed, cut in half*
>
> *3 cups Chinese cabbage, cut into 2-inch chunks*
>
> *3 to 6 Tablespoons chicken broth or water*

Mix chicken meat with cornstarch and stir fry sauce. Set aside.

Heat 2 Tablespoons cooking oil in stir fry pan or wok over medium-high heat. Add ginger, and stir fry 30 seconds. Add scallions, bamboo shoots, mushrooms and cabbage; continue stirring. Add chicken broth or water to pan and cover. Cook for 2 minutes, stirring occasionally. Remove vegetables to shallow bowl.

Heat remaining 2 Tablespoons oil in stir fry pan over medium-high heat. When oil is hot, add chicken mixture and stir fry until almost done, about 2 minutes. Return vegetables to pan and mix to combine meat and vegetables. Serve hot.

Yield: 4 to 6 servings

Variation: Use China Village Spicy Lemon Stir Fry Sauce

STEAMED CURRIED CHICKEN

Spoon this hearty stew into bowls of steaming rice or cooked noodles.

2 Tablespoons China Village Szechuan Stir Fry Sauce

1 Tablespoon dry sherry

1 slice ginger root, crushed

½ teaspoon curry paste or powder

2 minced scallions, divided

¾ pound chicken breast, skinned, boned and cut into ¾-inch cubes

1 medium carrot, peeled and cut into thin diagonal slices

1 Tablespoon cornstarch

2 Tablespoons water

Salt and black pepper, to taste

Combine stir fry sauce, sherry, ginger root, curry paste and half the scallions in an 8-inch round baking pan. Add chicken; stir until well coated. Arrange carrot slices over chicken.

In a stir fry pan or wok, bring water to boil. Place baking pan on a steamer rack; cover. Place over boiling water; cook 15 minutes or until chicken is done. Remove steamer rack from stir fry pan. With a slotted spoon, remove chicken and carrot slices to a serving bowl, reserving pan juices.

In a small cup, combine cornstarch and water.

Combine pan juices and cornstarch mixture in a medium saucepan. Bring to a boil, stirring constantly, until thickened. Add salt and pepper to taste. Pour sauce over chicken. Sprinkle with remaining scallions. Serve hot.

Yield: 3 to 4 servings

CHINA VILLAGE

SEAFOOD

DISHES

SEAFOOD MEDLEY IN CRISPY NOODLE NEST

If you prefer, serve this seafood stir fry in a nest of colorful leaf lettuce or ornamental kale.

1 recipe Bird's Nest Noodles, page 42
¾ pound medium raw shrimp, shelled and deveined
¼ pound sea scallops, cut into coins, or whole bay scallops
2 Tablespoons dry sherry, divided
1 teaspoon grated ginger root
1 Tablespoon China Village Spicy Lemon Stir Fry Sauce
3 Tablespoons chicken broth
1 teaspoon cornstarch
½ teaspoon sugar
4 Tablespoons China Village Garlic & Ginger Stir Fry Oil, divided
1 small red bell pepper, cubed
4 small black mushrooms, soaked, stems removed and cut in half
2 thin scallions, cut into 1-inch lengths
⅛ pound fresh pea pods, stems and strings removed
½ cup canned whole baby corn, drained and rinsed well

Prepare Bird's Nest Noodles as directed on page 42. Arrange on a large platter to form a nest; set aside.

Marinate shrimp and scallops in 1 Tablespoon sherry and ginger root.

In a small bowl, combine stir fry sauce, chicken broth, remaining 1 Tablespoon sherry, cornstarch and sugar; set aside.

Heat 1 Tablespoon oil in a stir fry pan or wok over medium-high heat. Stir fry bell pepper and mushrooms 2 minutes. Add scallions and pea pods; cook 1 minute. Add baby corn; cook 30 seconds. Remove vegetables to a plate.

Heat remaining 3 Tablespoons oil in stir fry pan. Stir fry shrimp and scallops 1 minute or until shrimp turn pink. Stir in sauce. Cook 1 minute until sauce thickens and seafood is cooked. Gently stir in vegetables until coated with sauce. Pour into noodle nest. Serve hot.

Yield: 4 to 5 servings
Variation: Use China Village Szechuan Stir Fry Sauce

BIRD'S NEST NOODLES

Wiry bean thread noodles puff up magically as they are fried. Use as a nest or garnish for Chinese dishes. Delicate rice stick noodles can be fried the same way. They are often tossed into salads.

vegetable oil for deep-frying
4 ounces bean threads (saifun) or rice sticks (maifun)

To separate the noodles neatly before frying, tear them apart inside a large paper bag. Or, use scissors to snip the bean threads into short pieces.

Pour 2 inches of oil into a stir fry pan or wok and heat over medium-high heat to 375°. To test the temperature, drop a strand of noodle in hot oil. If the noodle puffs up immediately, oil is ready.

Fry noodles in small portions, turning each portion to allow all the noodles to expand. Drain on paper towels.

Use within 4 or 5 hours for the freshest flavor.

Yield: One large noodle "nest"

SZECHUAN SHRIMP WITH PEA PODS

This dish is wonderful to look at and delicious to eat. The juicy, tender shrimp contrast beautifully with the crisp, green pea pods.

1 pound raw medium shrimp, shelled and deveined
3 Tablespoons China Village Szechuan Stir Fry Sauce
2 teaspoons cornstarch
2 Tablespoons China Village Garlic & Ginger Stir Fry Oil
chicken broth or water, as needed to thin sauce
¼ pound fresh pea pods, stems and strings removed
1 can (5 ounces) sliced water chestnuts, drained

Mix shrimp with stir fry sauce and cornstarch.

Heat oil in stir fry pan or wok over medium-high heat. Add shrimp mixture and stir fry for 2 minutes, or until shrimp are no longer translucent. Add 1 to 3 Tablespoons water or broth if mixture becomes too thick.

Add pea pods and water chestnuts, and stir fry for 2 minutes. Serve hot.

Yield: 4 to 6 servings
Variation: Use China Village Spicy Lemon Stir Fry Sauce

SHRIMP WITH LOBSTER SAUCE

The name is a bit misleading since there is no lobster in this dish, but it is the same kind of sauce the Cantonese serve with lobster.

1 pound raw medium shrimp, shelled and deveined
2 teaspoons dry sherry
2 Tablespoons cornstarch, divided
1¼ cups cold water, divided
4 Tablespoons cooking oil
2 slices ginger root
2 cloves garlic, crushed
1½ Tablespoons black beans, minced
½ cup ground pork (about ¼ pound)
½ teaspoon salt
2 Tablespoons soy sauce
¼ teaspoon sugar
1 egg, beaten

Combine shrimp with sherry and ½ Tablespoon cornstarch.

In a small bowl, stir the remaining 1½ Tablespoons cornstarch into ¼ cup cold water.

Heat oil in stir fry pan or wok over medium-high heat. Add shrimp mixture and stir fry for 2 minutes, or until shrimp are no longer translucent. Remove shrimp from pan, leaving as much oil as possible in the pan.

Return pan to heat. Add ginger root, garlic and black beans. Stir fry 30 seconds, then add pork, salt, soy sauce, sugar and 1 cup water. Bring to a boil. Cover and simmer for 2 minutes. Stir cornstarch mixture and add to pan, stirring well. Add shrimp and stir. Add beaten egg with one or two stirs. Serve hot.

Yield: 4 to 6 servings

LEMON SCALLOP STIR FRY

Small, sweet bay scallops are preferred for this dish. If you use the larger sea scallops, be sure to remove the small tough ligament and cut the scallops in half or thirds.

1 pound fresh bay scallops

1 teaspoon cornstarch

3 Tablespoons China Village Spicy Lemon Stir Fry Sauce

2 Tablespoons China Village Garlic & Ginger Stir Fry Oil or cooking oil

1 slice ginger root

¼ cup black mushrooms, soaked, stems removed and cut in half

¼ pound fresh pea pods, stems and strings removed, cut in half diagonally

Mix scallops with cornstarch and stir fry sauce. Set aside.

Heat 2 Tablespoons oil in stir fry pan or wok over medium-high heat. Add ginger root and stir fry 30 seconds. Add black mushrooms and stir fry 30 seconds, then add scallop mixture and cook for about 1 minute, stirring constantly, or until done.

Add pea pods and stir fry for another 30 seconds. Serve hot.

Yield: 4 to 6 servings

Variation: Use China Village Szechuan Stir Fry Sauce

PAN-FRIED SALMON WITH SPICY LEMON SAUCE

Butter and spicy lemon stir fry sauce blend to make a wonderful sauce for grilled fish. You can substitute pink trout for the salmon, if you prefer.

2 pieces of salmon fillets, ½ pound each

4 Tablespoons China Village Spicy Lemon Stir Fry Sauce, divided

2 Tablespoons dry sherry

2 thin slices ginger root, crushed

2 Tablespoons China Village Garlic & Ginger Stir Fry Oil

1 Tablespoon butter

2 Tablespoons fresh lemon juice

1 Tablespoon minced fresh cilantro

4 thin lemon slices

Place salmon fillets in a shallow glass dish. Add 2 Tablespoons of the stir fry sauce, sherry and ginger root. (At this point, the dish can be tightly wrapped and the salmon refrigerated several hours.)

Heat 2 Tablespoons garlic and ginger stir fry oil in a non-stick stir fry pan or large skillet over medium-high heat. Remove salmon from marinade; shake off excess liquid. Pan-fry the salmon 3 to 4 minutes on each side, or until fish turns pink and just begins to flake. Remove to serving plates.

Swirl butter, lemon juice, remaining 2 Tablespoons stir fry sauce and cilantro in the hot pan. Pour over salmon fillets. Garnish with lemon slices. Serve hot.

Yield: 2 servings

Variation: Use China Village Szechuan Stir Fry Sauce

SZECHUAN CLAMS WITH BLACK BEAN SAUCE

Clams must be absolutely fresh—buy only those with shells tightly shut. Be sure to soak and clean the clams thoroughly to rid them of all sand and grit. When cooked, the clam shells open and resemble the shape of silver ingots used in old China. That's why clams are often served during Chinese New Year to symbolize wealth for the coming year.

12 littleneck or cherrystone clams (about 2 pounds)

2 Tablespoons China Village Garlic & Ginger Stir Fry Oil or cooking oil

2 cloves garlic, crushed

2 slices ginger

1 stalk scallion, cut into 1-inch lengths

1 Tablespoon black beans, rinsed and coarsely chopped

½ cup water

2 Tablespoons China Village Szechuan Stir Fry Sauce

2 teaspoons cornstarch

1 Tablespoon water

1 Tablespoon minced coriander, as garnish

Cover clams in cool fresh water and soak for about 30 minutes. Scrub shells with brush, rinse thoroughly and drain.

Heat oil in stir fry pan or wok over medium-high heat. Add garlic, ginger, scallions and black beans. Stir fry for a few seconds until fragrant.

Add clams and stir for 30 seconds. Add stir fry sauce and ½ cup water; stir to mix. Lower heat to medium, and cover. Cook for approximately 5 minutes, or until clam shells open. Meanwhile, combine 2 teaspoons cornstarch with 1 Tablespoon water.

Remove lid and add cornstarch mixture, stirring constantly until sauce is thickened. Transfer clams and sauce to platter and sprinkle with minced coriander. Serve immediately.

Yield: 4 servings

STEAMED WHOLE FISH

A whole fish makes a dramatic presentation, although you may use fish fillets. Whether you use sea bass, striped bass, flounder, red snapper or rock cod, always be sure the fish is absolutely fresh.

1 whole fish or fish fillets (about 2 pounds)
1 stalk scallion, shredded
1 Tablespoon shredded fresh ginger root
2 Tablespoons China Village Spicy Lemon Stir Fry Sauce
1½ Tablespoons cooking oil
1 teaspoon sesame oil
3 Tablespoons minced coriander, as garnish

If using a whole fish, scale and clean thoroughly. Rinse. Score both sides of fish with long, diagonal, parallel cuts, almost to the bone. This allows flavors to properly penetrate fish and cook more evenly. Put fish in shallow platter or pie plate. (If the fish is too long, cut it in half.)

Spread shredded scallion and ginger over fish and pour stir fry sauce evenly over the top.

Place water in a steamer and bring to a boil. Place the plate with fish in the steamer. Cover and cook over medium-high heat for about 10 to 15 minutes, or until flesh at the thickest part turns white.

When fish is almost done, heat cooking oil and sesame oil in stir fry pan or small saucepan over medium-high heat until hot but not smoking. Remove fish from steamer and scatter chopped fresh coriander over fish. Carefully pour hot oil over fish, and serve immediately.

Yield: 4 to 6 servings
Variation: Use China Village Szechuan Stir Fry Sauce

RED SNAPPER WITH BROCCOLI AND BLACK MUSHROOMS

If you don't have snapper, you can substitute other fish fillets such as sea bass, Pacific cod, catfish or haddock.

¾ pound Atlantic red snapper fillets, cut into 1½-inch squares

2 Tablespoons dry sherry

¼ cup chicken broth

2 Tablespoons China Village Szechuan Stir Fry Sauce

1 Tablespoon oyster sauce

1½ teaspoons cornstarch

½ pound broccoli florets

3 medium black mushrooms, soaked, stems removed and quartered

2 scallions, cut diagonally in 1-inch pieces

4 Tablespoons China Village Garlic & Ginger Stir Fry Oil, divided

1 teaspoon grated ginger root

1 clove garlic, minced

Place fish in a large bowl; add sherry. In a small bowl, combine chicken broth, stir fry sauce, oyster sauce and cornstarch; set aside.

Plunge broccoli into boiling water for 1 minute to blanch. Remove to a bowl of iced water. Drain well and pat dry with paper towels. Place on a platter with mushrooms and scallions.

Heat 1 Tablespoon oil in a stir fry pan or wok over medium-high heat. Stir fry broccoli, mushrooms and scallion 1 minute. Remove to platter.

Heat 3 Tablespoons oil in stir fry pan. Add ginger, garlic and fish; stir fry 1 minute. Stir broth mixture and pour into pan. Cook 1 minute until thickened. Add vegetables, and gently stir until everything is coated with sauce. Pour onto serving platter. Serve hot.

Yield: 3 to 4 servings

Variation: Use China Village Spicy Lemon Stir Fry Sauce

CHINA VILLAGE

VEGETABLES

AND

SALADS

STIR-FRIED CHINESE CABBAGE

The leaves, leaf stalks and flowering shoots of Chinese bok choy are edible. Excellent for stir frying, this cabbage has a clean, refreshing taste.

1 pound Chinese cabbage

½ teaspoon sugar

1 Tablespoon China Village Szechuan Stir Fry Sauce

1 Tablespoon rice vinegar

2 Tablespoons China Village Garlic & Ginger Stir Fry Oil

2 slices ginger root, crushed

⅓ cup finely shredded country-style ham

½ teaspoon Mexican Fiesta Chile Pepper Oil, or to taste

salt, to taste

Separate leaf stalks of cabbage. Rinse and trim off any discolored outer leaves. Cut stems and leaves in half lengthwise. Cut crosswise into 1½-inch pieces. In a small bowl, combine sugar, stir fry sauce and vinegar.

Heat oil in a stir fry pan or wok over medium-high heat. Add ginger. Stir fry 1 minute; discard ginger. Add ham and stir fry 15 seconds. Add cabbage. Stir fry 2 minutes.

Sprinkle in sauce mixture. Stir fry 2 to 3 minutes or just until crisp-tender. Drizzle in chile pepper oil. Remove from heat. If necessary, salt to taste. Serve at once.

Yield: 3 to 4 servings

BEAN SPROUT, HAM AND CARROT SALAD

The bean sprout mixture and dressing can be prepared ahead and refrigerated separately. Do not combine until serving time.

¾ pound bean sprouts

2 ounces thinly sliced baked ham, shredded

1 carrot, shredded

2 Tablespoons China Village Szechuan Stir Fry Sauce

2 Tablespoons rice vinegar

1 teaspoon sugar
1 teaspoon sesame oil

Put bean sprouts in a large colander. Bring 6 cups water to boil; pour over sprouts. Immediately place sprouts into a bowl of iced water to chill. Drain well. Pat dry with paper towels.

In a large bowl, toss bean sprouts with shredded ham and carrot. Combine remaining ingredients in a small bowl. Pour over bean sprout mixture. Toss well. Serve at once.

Yield: 4 to 6 servings

SZECHUAN SPICED EGGPLANT

If the eggplant is fresh and has a thin tender skin, it is not necessary to peel it.

2 small eggplants (about 1½ pounds)
3 Tablespoons China Village Garlic & Ginger Stir Fry Oil
1 stalk scallion, minced
1 slice ginger root
½ cup chicken broth or water
4 Tablespoons China Village Szechuan Stir Fry Sauce
1 Tablespoon cornstarch
2 Tablespoons water

Cut stems off eggplants and remove skin. Cut into wedges, then into 2-inch chunks.

Heat oil in stir fry pan or wok over medium-high heat. Add scallion and ginger, stir frying for about 20 seconds.

Add eggplant and stir fry for about 2 minutes. Add ½ cup chicken broth or water and continue cooking, covered, for about 2 minutes or until tender. Add more liquid as necessary. Add stir fry sauce, and stir a few times.

Combine cornstarch and water, and stir into dish. Continue stirring until sauce thickens. Serve hot.

Yield: 4 to 6 servings

STIR-FRIED VEGETABLE MEDLEY

Here is a great way to eat your daily quota of vegetables!

3 Tablespoons China Village Garlic & Ginger Stir Fry Oil, divided

1 clove garlic, minced

1 teaspoon grated ginger root

6 black mushrooms, soaked, stems removed, quartered

¼ pound fresh pea pods (about 2 cups), stems and strings removed

½ medium cauliflower, separated into florets

1 large carrot, sliced diagonally, ¼-inch thick

¼ cup chicken broth

1 Tablespoon China Village Szechuan Stir Fry Sauce

salt, to taste

Heat 1½ Tablespoons oil in a stir fry pan or wok over medium-high heat. Stir fry garlic, ginger and mushrooms 30 seconds. Add pea pods. Stir fry 1 minute or until crisp-tender. Remove to a platter.

Heat 1½ Tablespoons oil in stir fry pan. Stir fry cauliflower 1 minute. Add carrot; cook 1 minute. Add broth and stir fry sauce. Reduce heat. Cover and cook 2 to 3 minutes or until vegetables are crisp-tender.

Remove lid. Cook 1 minute, or until most of the liquid evaporates. Stir in mushroom mixture. If necessary, add salt, to taste. Remove to serving platter. Serve hot.

Yield: 3 to 4 servings

STEAMED EGGPLANT SALAD

This dish is wonderful for the summer as it can be served cold. It is a time-saver as well since it can be prepared ahead of time. If your eggplants are young and tender, there is no need to remove the skin.

2 small eggplants (about 1 pound)

3 Tablespoons cider vinegar

3 Tablespoons light brown sugar

2 teaspoons sesame oil

1 Tablespoon soy sauce

1 Tablespoon ginger root, grated
1 teaspoon garlic, finely minced

Remove stems from eggplants and peel off skin. Cut eggplant into six or eight wedges. Spread the wedges on a steamer or steaming basket. (The juice of the eggplant is bitter so using a perforated steaming basket will permit the bitter juice to drain out as it cooks.)

Steam eggplants for 8 to 10 minutes over high heat, or until tender. (Test for tenderness by piercing the eggplants with a fork—eggplants are ready when they are easily pierced.) Place eggplants on a serving dish.

In a small shaker jar combine the vinegar, brown sugar, sesame oil, soy sauce, ginger and garlic; mix well. Pour over eggplant, mix well and serve.

Yield: 4 to 6 servings

STIR-FRIED "KAN SHAO" GREEN BEANS

This is an easy and tasty side dish to accompany a meal.

1 pound green beans
2 Tablespoons China Village Garlic & Ginger Stir Fry Oil or
*   cooking oil*
1 Tablespoon black beans, rinsed and coarsely chopped
½ cup chicken broth
1 Tablespoon China Village Szechuan Stir Fry Sauce

Snap the ends off the beans and cut into 2-inch lengths. Rinse in cold water and drain well.

Heat oil in stir fry pan or wok over medium-high heat. Add black beans, and stir fry for 15 seconds. Add green beans and stir fry for about 30 seconds.

Add broth and cook covered for about 3 to 5 minutes or until tender-crisp. Stir occasionally. Remove lid, and turn heat to high. Add stir fry sauce, and stir constantly for another minute until the liquid is almost gone. Serve immediately.

Yield: 4 to 6 servings

FRIED BEAN CURD WITH BROCCOLI

Pan-fried bean curd has a delightfully firm skin, with soft bean curd inside. It contrasts well with the tender-crisp vegetables. Stir and handle the bean curd gently so it doesn't break.

1 cake firm bean curd (about 1 pound)

1 small bunch broccoli (about 2 cups florets)

5 Tablespoons China Village Garlic & Ginger Stir Fry Oil, divided

3 Tablespoons water or chicken broth

1 small can sliced bamboo shoots, drained

3 Tablespoons China Village Szechuan Stir Fry Sauce

2 teaspoons cornstarch

1 Tablespoon water

Pat bean curd dry with paper towels. Cut into 12 to 16 pieces, each approximately 2 inches by ¾ inch by 1 inch. Set aside.

Cut broccoli into 1½-inch florets. Peel stems and cut into same size lengths, about ½ inch thick.

Heat 4 Tablespoons oil in stir fry pan or wok over medium-high heat and swish oil to cover sides. Add bean curd in a single layer and fry until bottom turns golden brown. Gently turn with spatula to brown the second side. Remove bean curd from pan, leaving behind as much oil as possible, and drain on paper towels. Remove pan from heat.

Add remaining 1 Tablespoon oil to stir fry pan over medium-high heat. Add broccoli and stir fry until it turns a dark green. Add 3 Tablespoons water or broth and lower heat to medium. Cover and steam broccoli for 2 to 3 minutes. If water evaporates before desired tenderness is reached, add more water.

Remove cover; add bamboo shoots and fried bean curd. Pour in stir fry sauce and gently stir fry for about 30 seconds to mix. Combine cornstarch and water and add to pan, stirring until sauce thickens. Serve immediately.

Yield: 4 to 6 servings

LEMON CUCUMBER SALAD

For a spicier taste, substitute 1 teaspoon China Village Garlic & Ginger Stir Fry Oil for the sesame oil.

1 European cucumber or 2 medium regular cucumbers, peeled
⅓ cup white vinegar
1 Tablespoon sugar
1½ teaspoons China Village Szechuan Stir Fry Sauce
1 teaspoon sesame oil
1 teaspoon black or white sesame seeds, as garnish

Cut cucumber in half lengthwise. With a small spoon, scrape out and discard any seeds. Cut cucumber halves crosswise into ¼-inch slices.

In a medium bowl, whisk together vinegar, sugar, stir fry sauce and sesame oil. Add cucumber slices; mix well. Marinate 15 minutes. Place in a serving dish and sprinkle with sesame seeds. Serve at once or refrigerate up to an hour.

Yield: 4 to 6 servings

FRESH ASPARAGUS SALAD

Cut off the white and tough parts of the asparagus and remove the lower little leaves. Asparagus can be sandy, so wash it very carefully.

1 small bunch fresh asparagus
3 Tablespoons soy sauce
1 teaspoon sesame oil

Wash and drain. Roll cut the asparagus into 1½-inch lengths.

Bring 6 cups water to a boil in a large pot over high heat. Parboil the asparagus by plunging it into the boiling water. When the water boils again, drain and plunge into cold water until the asparagus is thoroughly cold. Drain well.

To serve, toss the asparagus with the soy sauce and drizzle with sesame oil. Mix well.

Yield: 4 servings

CRUNCHY CHINESE CHICKEN SALAD

This salad is especially tasty if made with the Chinese Roast Chicken on page 33.

2 cups hand-shredded roasted chicken

1 recipe Bird's Nest Noodles, page 42 (use 4 ounces rice sticks)

4 Tablespoons China Village Szechuan Stir Fry Sauce

3 Tablespoons rice vinegar

3 Tablespoons fresh lemon juice

2 Tablespoons sugar

2 Tablespoons safflower or canola oil

½ teaspoon grated ginger root

4 cups shredded lettuce

3 scallions, shredded

½ cucumber, seeded, cut in julienne strips

⅓ cup torn cilantro leaves

1 Tablespoon toasted sesame seeds

½ cup toasted pine nuts, as garnish

Hand-shred roasted chicken to equal 2 cups. Set aside.

Fry noodles according to directions on page 42. Set aside.

To make dressing, whisk together the stir fry sauce, vinegar, lemon juice, sugar, oil and ginger.

Layer the shredded lettuce, scallions, cucumber, cilantro, chicken and noodles in a large bowl. Sprinkle with sesame seeds. Add dressing, as needed, to coat salad. Carefully mix ingredients. Arrange portions on serving plates. Sprinkle with pine nuts. Pass remaining dressing. Serve at once.

Yield: 3 to 4 servings

Variation: Use China Village Spicy Lemon Stir Fry Sauce

CHINA VILLAGE

NOODLES,

RICE

AND

DUMPLINGS

STIR FRIED NOODLES WITH SHREDDED PORK

Also known as lo mein, noodles made from wheat flour are popular in Northern China, where it is too cold to grow rice.

½ pound Chinese-style fresh noodles

½ cup lean pork, shredded

3 Tablespoons China Village Szechuan Stir Fry Sauce

1 teaspoon cornstarch

4 Tablespoons China Village Garlic & Ginger Stir Fry Oil or cooking oil

½ cup canned bamboo shoots, drained and shredded

½ cup black mushrooms, soaked and shredded

½ cup fresh pea pods, shredded

¼ cup scallions, shredded

Cook and prepare noodles according to package directions. Be careful not to overcook. Drain and rinse in cold water.

Mix pork with stir fry sauce and cornstarch.

Heat oil in a stir fry pan or wok over medium-high heat. Add shredded pork mixture and stir fry for about 1 minute. Add shredded bamboo shoots, black mushrooms, pea pods and scallions. Stir fry for 1 to 2 minutes.

Add cooked noodles, and mix until noodles are heated and ingredients are thoroughly mixed together. Serve hot.

Yield: 4 servings

CHINESE SOUP NOODLES WITH SLICED BEEF

A hot and delicious one-dish meal or snack. Great on a cold, winter day. Substitute spinach for the cabbage, if you prefer.

1 pound Chinese noodles
½ pound flank steak
3 Tablespoons China Village Szechuan Stir Fry Sauce
1 teaspoon cornstarch
1 Tablespoon cooking oil
2 slices ginger root
2 stalks scallions, cut into 1½-inch sections
1 can (13¾ ounces) beef broth
1 cup water
½ pound chopped napa, bok choy, or Chinese cabbage
minced coriander and sesame oil, as garnish

Cook noodles according to package directions. Drain and rinse in cold water.

Cut beef into thin ¼-inch slices about 2 inches by 1½ inches. Mix beef with stir fry sauce and cornstarch. Set aside.

Heat oil in stir fry pan or wok over medium-high heat. Add ginger root and scallions, and stir fry for about 30 to 45 seconds. Add beef mixture and stir for another 1 to 2 minutes. Add beef broth and water, stir and bring to a boil. Reduce heat to medium and add cabbage. Cover and allow to simmer for 2 to 3 minutes. Remove from heat.

Divide noodles into 4 large serving bowls. Ladle broth with the meat and vegetables on top. Garnish each serving with minced coriander and ¼ teaspoon sesame oil. Serve steaming hot.

Note: If you prefer spicy noodles, substitute Mexican Fiesta Chile Pepper Oil for the sesame oil.

Variation: Substitute shredded chicken breast and chicken broth to make Chinese Soup Noodles with Chicken.

Yield: 4 main course servings

COLD SPICED CHINESE NOODLES

Also known as "Dan Dan Mien," this is a wonderful summer lunch or picnic dish. You may vary the garnishes by using ham, pork, turkey or other cooked meat. Shredded radishes, carrots, chives or other vegetables may also be used.

1 pound Chinese noodles

3 Tablespoons sesame oil, divided

½ cup smooth peanut butter

½ cup chicken broth, divided

3 Tablespoons China Village Szechuan Stir Fry Sauce

1 teaspoon Mexican Fiesta Chile Pepper Oil, or to taste

GARNISHES
(use one or all)

2 cups hand-shredded roasted chicken

1 small cucumber, partially peeled, seeded, finely shredded

1½ cups bean sprouts, parboiled, rinsed in cold water and drained

3 Tablespoons white sesame seeds, lightly toasted

Cook noodles according to package directions. Do not overcook. Drain, rinse with cold water, drain again and toss with 1 Tablespoon sesame oil. Set aside.

To make the sauce: Combine peanut butter and ¼ cup chicken broth in small bowl. Mix until liquid is absorbed, then stir in remainder of broth until mixture forms a smooth thin paste, with the consistency of syrup. Blend in stir fry sauce, remainder of sesame oil and chile oil. Set aside. (This may be done in a blender or food processor.)

To assemble dish: Place chilled noodles in large serving bowl. Pour peanut sauce over noodles, and toss well with chopsticks or two large forks. Decorate top with garnish of shredded chicken and vegetables. Sprinkle with sesame seeds and serve.

Yield: 3 to 4 main course servings

ALMOND FRIED RICE

Authentic fried rice is never stained dark with soy sauce. If you like, sprinkle in a few drops of China Village Szechuan Stir Fry Sauce for an untraditional, yet wonderful flavor.

4 cups cooked long-grain rice, prepared ahead and chilled
4 Tablespoons China Village Garlic & Ginger Stir Fry Oil,
   divided
2 large eggs, lightly beaten
4 thin scallions, thinly sliced
1 large clove garlic, minced
½ cup frozen peas, thawed
⅓ cup toasted, slivered almonds or pine nuts
salt, to taste

Place chilled rice in a large bowl, and break up any clumps with a fork.

Heat 1 Tablespoon oil in a nonstick stir fry pan or wok over medium-high heat. Scramble eggs until set, yet still soft. Remove to a platter. Wipe any remaining egg from pan, if necessary.

Heat 3 Tablespoons oil in stir fry pan over medium-high heat. Stir fry scallions and garlic 30 seconds. Add rice. Stir fry for 3 minutes, or until rice is heated through. Add peas; stir fry 1 minute.

Add scrambled eggs to rice. Stir in almonds, mixing well to combine the ingredients. Add salt, to taste. Serve hot.

Yield: 3 to 4 servings

SPICY MEAT-FILLED DUMPLINGS

Simmered in broth, these dumplings are much lower in fat than fried dumplings.

1 recipe Szechuan Dipping Sauce, page 63

FILLING MIXTURE

1 pound lean ground pork or beef
½ cup minced, tender cabbage leaves
3 Tablespoons China Village Szechuan Stir Fry Sauce
3 Tablespoons dry sherry or water
1 Tablespoon minced fresh ginger root
2 green onions, minced
½ teaspoon sesame oil
¼ teaspoon ground black pepper

1 egg
½ pound fresh wonton skins (about 36)
cornstarch, as needed to dust tray
2 Tablespoons chicken-flavored bouillon granules

Prepare Szechuan Dipping Sauce as directed on page 63. Set aside. In a medium bowl, combine ingredients for filling. In a small bowl, beat the egg.

To make a dumpling, place a wonton skin on a dumpling press. Place 1 teaspoon filling in the center of the skin. Moisten edges with egg. Close the press tightly to seal. Remove dumpling from mold. Place on a tray lightly dusted with cornstarch. Keep lightly covered.

In a large pot, bring 3 quarts water and 2 Tablespoons chicken bouillon granules to a boil. Add one-third of the dumplings. Reduce heat; simmer 1 to 2 minutes. Dumplings will float when done. With a slotted spoon, remove to serving platter. Keep warm; cook remaining dumplings. Serve warm with dipping sauce.

Yield: 12 appetizer servings

Variation: Dumplings can be deep-fried in hot oil until crisp and golden brown. Serve with China Village Sweet & Sour Dipping Sauce on the side.

SZECHUAN DIPPING SAUCE

Use as a dipping sauce for dumplings, meatballs or savory pastries.

⅓ cup China Village Szechuan Stir Fry Sauce
4 Tablespoons rice vinegar
½ teaspoon sugar
½ teaspoon sesame oil
1 large garlic clove, minced
1 teaspoon Mexican Fiesta Chile Pepper Oil, or to taste
1 scallion, minced

In a medium bowl, combine all the ingredients and stir well to combine. Allow to sit at room temperature 30 minutes for flavors to develop.

Yield: About ⅔ cup

NOODLES TOSSED WITH SPICY BEEF

The poetic name of this Chinese dish is Ants Climbing a Tree. It is supposed to remind us of ants climbing up the branches of a tree. Kids love noodles with ground meat. For them, you may want to reduce the amount of chile pepper oil.

3 ounces mung bean noodles
½ cup chicken broth
2 Tablespoons China Village Szechuan Stir Fry Sauce
2 Tablespoons dry sherry
1 teaspoons Mexican Fiesta Chile Pepper Oil, or to taste
3 Tablespoons China Village Garlic & Ginger Stir Fry Oil
1 large clove garlic, minced
1 Tablespoon minced ginger root
3 scallions, minced
½ pound lean ground beef, pork or turkey
salt, to taste

Soak noodles in hot water for 20 minutes. Drain well. Cut noodles into shorter, more manageable lengths.

In a small bowl, combine chicken broth, stir fry sauce, sherry and chile oil; set aside.

Heat 3 Tablespoons stir fry oil in a stir fry pan or wok over medium-high heat. Stir fry garlic, ginger and two-thirds of the scallions for 1 minute.

Add meat. Cook until broken up and no longer pink. Stir in sauce. Add noodles. Toss ingredients together. Reduce heat slightly. Cook, turning ingredients, until liquid evaporates and flavors blend together. If necessary, add salt to taste. Remove to serving platter. Garnish with reserved scallions. Serve hot.

Yield: 3 to 4 servings